Book

The Kianap

Reading Practice

pat	damp
kid	pest
rob	risk
cut	loft
pet	tuft
lob	bunk
fed	felt
jab	limp
pit	bolt
mop	cult
lit	sand
nut	tend
jet	silk
ban	jolt
mud	bulk

At the bottom of each page of text, some multisyllable words are split up for the reader.

Contents

Chapter 1   "Get Up!"   page 1

Chapter 2   Dusk   page 5

Chapter 3   The Wagon   page 8

Chapter 4   An Odd Feeling   page 11

Vocabulary:

jab	– poke roughly
fed up	– annoyed or bored
lulls	– calms or soothes
sobs	– cries with gasping noises
jolts	– moves with sudden, sharp movements
feels odd	– feels strange

Chapter 1
"Get Up!"

"Zak! Get up!" Grandpa gives Zak a jab. "Zak! The sun is up. You must get up!" "Must I?" Zak sits up.

Grand pa

Zak nods off. "The sun is up. You must get on," Grandpa says. "You must keep the kid with you." Zak nods, "Yes."

Grand pa

Zak sets off. He kicks up dust as he runs. The kid is in a bag on his back. "This job is not fun," says Zak to himself.

him self

Zak gets to a hill. He lets the kid run off into the soft grass. Zak cuts his staff with his dagger. He is fed up.

in to   da gger

Chapter 2
Dusk

"I will tell Grandpa I'm fed up with this job," Zak says to himself. The wind lulls him to sleep. He sits on the soft grass and has a nap.

Grand pa   him self

Zak gets up with a jolt. It is dusk. The sun has set. "Where is the kid?" Zak jumps up. Grandpa will be so cross!

Grand pa

As he runs back, he can see a wagon. Two men rest next to it. The big man has the kid. Zak is upset. This is bad.

wa gon　　up set

Chapter 3
The Wagon

"That's my pet kid!" Zak says. The man will not give Zak the kid. "Get the lad! We can sell him as well!" the big man yells.

The man grabs Zak and locks him in the wagon. A girl is in the wagon as well. She must be ten. The girl sobs.

wa gon

"Did they kidnap you?" the girl asks. "Yes," Zak nods. The wagon jolts as it sets off.

kid nap

Chapter 4
An Odd Feeling

The wagon jogs on and on and on. Zak is sad. Will Grandpa send for help? Then Zak feels odd. Someone else is in the wagon!

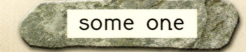
some one

An old woman is sitting next to him. Is she bad? Can she help him? Can she help him get back to Grandpa?

wo man — sitt ing